Journey to Resurrection Day
3 weeks of lessons
leading up to and including Palm Sunday and Easter
Building Foundations: A Spirit-Filled Children's Church Curriculum

Pastor Tamera Kraft
Revival Fire 4 Kids Resource

Mt Zion Ridge Press
http://mtzionridgepress.com
Managing Editors: Michelle L. Levigne and Tamera Lynn Kraft
Cover Art: Tamera Lynn Kraft

ISBN 978-1-968693-19-0

Registration and Digital Files (Available for FREE with purchase of the curriculum): Digital files (jpeg graphics, video clips, other resources) are available to anyone who purchases and registers this curriculum at no additional cost. You can download the resources at a Dropbox link https://tinyurl.com/revivalfire-dropbox or using this QR Code.

Or you can register at this link http://eepurl.com/glsELH or type it in the address box on your browser and fill out the form. We never sell or give away any information we receive.

Journey to Resurrection Day is available in PDF download and paperback.

All Scripture in this curriculum is from the NIV (2011) Bible unless otherwise designated.

For questions about copyright issues or other matters concerning rights for this curriculum, contact revivalfire4kids@att.net.

Building Foundations Curriculum is a Revival Fire for Kids resource. For more information about Revival Fire for Kids, check out their website at http://revivalfire4kids.com.

Materials included:

3 complete downloadable lessons including 6 object lessons, 6 skits with video, 3 games, 3 Bible Stories, 3 memory verse activities, graphics to be used in PowerPoint slides for 3 lessons, 3 small group discussions or activities, and optional lessons and activities.

Lessons, graphics, videos, and Family Devotion Handouts will be available for immediate download upon registering this curriculum at this link: https://shorturl.at/gpUX8 or click on the QR code above.

How To Use This Curriculum:

Scriptural Premise: Students will learn the events leading up to the crucifixion and resurrection and come to the knowledge of how that allows them to have a relationship with God.

Week 1: Lazurus is raised from the dead (John 11:1-44)

Week 2: Jesus Enters Jerusalem (Matthew 21:1-17)

Week 3: Jesus dies, is buried, and rises again (Matthew 27:32 – 28:10)

Decorations: Decorations and set design should reflect Jerusalem during Bible times. You can use curtains to represent the temple. You can also use large appliance boxes for buildings and a cave. A picture will be provided with the curriculum resources you can use as a backdrop.

Italics: Italics are used for Scripture. They are also used in this curriculum for passages or speeches the teacher or worker may want to say in their own words. For skits, italics are only used to designate the person speaking.

 **Registration and Digital Files (Available for FREE with purchase of the curriculum):** Digital files (JPG graphics, video clips, other resources) are available to anyone who purchases and registers this curriculum at no additional cost at this QR Code.

You can also register to receive updates on curriculum, other resources, and news about Revival Fire for Kids. Click on this link http://eepurl.com/glsELH or type it in the address box on your browser and fill out the form to register. We never sell or give away any information we receive.

Welcome:

Opening: A slide and countdown will be provided for pre-service time. Fast music in the background is recommended.

Welcome: Each lesson will welcome the children with an introduction to that day's message.

Prayer: It's important to start each lesson with prayer.

Rules: A list of 5 Ups are included in the graphics available after registration. Rehearse the rules every week.

Theme Song: Get the kids up and moving at the beginning of every lesson with a fun theme song. Recommended theme song that will work with this curriculum are He's

Alive, He's Alive by Yancy, Jesus is Alive by Singing Praise Kids, or Christ is Risen From the Dead by God's Kids Worship.

Memory Verse: Every lesson has a memory verse. The verse will be included in a slide and will be illustrated in three ways. You can choose to use any of these illustrations to teach the verse, or you could use all three throughout your lesson.

Memory Verse Skit: A puppet skit video is included in each lesson to introduce the Memory Verse. Each puppet skit is available in the downloadable resources, and the skit is also available for churches that use puppets.

Memory Verse Talk: This is a short talk explaining what the verse means to the children. Memorizing God's Word is important, but it's more important for your students to know what a verse means.

Memory Verse Activity: Children learn by seeing, reading, hearing, and doing. The memory verse activity is a simple tool to help students remember the verse.

Game Time: A Game Time slide is included with registration for this curriculum. It isn't necessary to include a game with every week's lesson, but if you do, you should have a fun game that relates to the lesson. Game Time is the place for that. You may also want to save the game for last so, if the adult service runs long, you can play games until the parents arrive to retrieve their children.

Videos: Puppet skits, drama skits, and countdowns are available with Journey to Resurrection Day media resource downloads.

Offering: Lessons include a short talk on why children should give in the offering. You can expand the fun by having an offering contest with the boys against the girls. You can use a scale with buckets or have two offering plates and count the money. Once a month or once a quarter, have a special reward for the winning team.

Praise & Worship: Each week, a time of praise and worship is included to ready the students' hearts to hear the Word of God. This curriculum does not provide music because every church has different musical needs and tastes.

Lesson of the Week:

Bible Story: Each week, a Bible story skit is included. It has a skit for churches that use drama and video clips for churches without drama teams.

Object Lessons: At least two, sometimes three, object lessons illustrate the points of each week's lesson. Resources for the object lessons are not included.

Message: A short message ties up the lesson for the day and asks for a response from the students during altar ministry time.

Small Group Chat/Activity: Some children's ministries prefer to end each children's service with a small group chat, a small group Bible study, or a craft at some time during the week or use the activity before Children's Church begins. Small group chat questions, activities, and crafts are included for these purposes. Divide students into small groups of not more than six children. You can divide them by ages or include different ages together. Questions and instructions for activities are included to help the leader facilitate a chat with the students about the lesson. Small group sessions will help your students go home with practical applications for what they have learned.

Home Application: Each lesson will include a handout for the children to take home. Each handout will include this week's memory verse, a summary of the lesson, a Bible reading for each day, and a weekly family activity. This handout is available as a printable PDF download in our downloadable resources.

Scope and Sequence

Lesson 1: Lazurus is Raised from the Dead

Focus Point: Jesus gives us eternal life.

Goal: Students will learn that Jesus is stronger than death. When we follow Jesus, He gives us eternal life.

Verse of the Day: John 11:25 (NIV) *Jesus said…, "I am the resurrection and the life. The one who believes in me will live, even though they die;"*

Supplies Needed:

- Journey to Resurrection Day Media Resources
- Bible costumes for skit (optional)
- Product carrying lifetime guarantee
- Backpack
- Spray bottles and cleaning products
- Strips of construction paper in Easter colors
- Glue
- Marker board
- Eraser

Opening: Use Journey to Resurrection Day Slide or Countdown (Available free with registration of this curriculum.)

Welcome: Welcome the children and tell them how excited you are to see them. Ask them if they're excited about Resurrection Day. If they don't know what Resurrection Day is, let them know some people call it Easter. Tell them that for the next three weeks, they're going to take a journey back in time to when the first Resurrection Day happened. This week, they'll learn that Jesus has the power to raise people from the dead.

Prayer: Ask a child to pray over the service.

Rules: (use rules slide available in Journey to Resurrection Day Media Resources) Go over the 5 Ups Rules.

Go over the 5 Ups Rules:

- Sit up straight.
- Listen up.
- Hush up.
- Don't get up and run around or go to the bathroom without permission.
- Worship Up! (stand up and participate during praise and worship)

Theme or Activity Songs: Choose one or two fast-moving activity or theme songs that go with the curriculum.

Game Time: The Mummy Game (use game time slide)

Supplies Needed: 2-4 rolls of toilet paper

God wants everyone to live forever with Him in Heaven, but not everyone accepts God's gift of eternal life. Those who never ask God to forgive them of their sins are like mummies. They're spiritually dead, and yet, they still are walking around. Today we're going to learn about a man who died and was wrapped up like a mummy. But he didn't stay dead.

Depending on how many students there are, choose two to four teams of four people each. One child on each team will be the mummy. The other children will wrap the mummy in toilet paper. The mummy is not allowed to help by holding the toilet paper. The game begins when the music begins and ends when the music ends. The team with the best-wrapped mummy wins.

Offering: Giving Back

Each of you should give what you have decided in your heart to give, not reluctantly or under compulsion, for God loves a cheerful giver. *2 Corinthians 9:7 (NIV)*

Just like Lazarus *was raised to new* life, we *have* new life in *Christ* too *when we accept Him as our Savior*. And part of living that new life is giving cheerfully—whether it's money, time, or helping others.

So when you give your offering today, remember: You're giving because Jesus gave you new life!

Verse of the Day: John 11:25 (NIV) Jesus said…, "I am the resurrection and the life. The one who believes in me will live, even though they die;"

Memory Verse Skit: (Use media puppet skit resources)

Simon: (comes in sighing and acting sad, stops and acts startled when he sees boys and girls)

I didn't know you were going to be here. I was on the way to my Grandpa's funeral. My name's Simon, and my Grandpa's name is Simon too. I was named after him. But a couple of days ago, Grandpa Simon died and went to Heaven. (sighs loudly) I miss Grandpa Simon, but my mom says everyone dies. She says that's okay because if we love Jesus, we won't stay dead. We'll go to Heaven where we'll never die again. She says that's because of something Jesus said. Jesus is the Son of God and everything He says is true. In John 11: 25 : Jesus said…, "I am the resurrection and the life. The one who believes in me will live, even though they die;" He even raised His friend, Lazarus, from the dead to prove it. I prayed for Jesus to raise Grandpa from the dead too, but my mom said it was his time to go to Heaven. My Grandpa's body is dead, but he isn't really dead, not the real him. He's in Heaven with Jesus. I still miss him, but one day I'll see him again. I gotta go now. The funeral's starting soon. If you can all come back next week, I'll see you then. Bye.

Memory Verse Talk: (use Journey to Resurrection Day Lesson 1, slide 1)

John 11:25 is one of the most important verses in the Bible. Quote the verse, and have the children repeat it after you.

How many of you know somebody who died? (Allow the children to respond.) It's very sad when somebody we're close to dies. Most people don't die until they're very old, but someday everybody will die, hopefully a long time from now. It's very sad because we miss our grandparents and friends and family who have died.

But this verse gives us good news about death. Anyone who believes in Jesus, even though he will someday die, he won't really die. He'll go to Heaven to live forever with Jesus. That means, if we believe in Jesus, we'll see our loved ones again someday because we will have eternal life in Heaven.

Jesus can give us eternal life because He is the resurrection and the life. He is the Son of God and has power over life and death.

Memory Verse Activity: Erase a Word

Supplies needed: Marker board, eraser or Media Resource Slides lesson 1, slides 1-12

Write verse on a marker board. Have the students say the verse out loud. Then erase one word. Have the students repeat the verse. Then erase another word. Continue until all the words are erased.

Bible Story Skit: Jesus Raises Lazurus From the Dead (Use Journey to Resurrection Day Lesson One Bible Story Skit or have your drama team act this out.)

(John 11:1-44)

Supplies Needed (Optional): toilet paper, Bible costumes, cave

Narrator – Dressed in robe and turban
Jesus – Wears white robe
Lazarus – Rolled up in toilet paper and waiting in the cave

Narrator in robe and turban comes out.

Narrator: Hello boys and girls. Your children's pastor wanted me to tell you how Jesus is really stirring things up around here. I live in Jerusalem, but I went to visit some friends in Bethany a few days ago. Bethany's only a couple of miles outside of Jerusalem, so I visit them often. My friends told me a neighbor of theirs had died. This man, Lazarus was a friend of Jesus, that prophet who's been going around teaching about God and healing people. I heard about Him but I never met Him.
Anyway, Lazarus had died, and Jesus didn't even come to the funeral. Lazarus' sisters, Martha and Mary, were pretty upset about it. They said something I didn't understand about how if Jesus had been there, their brother wouldn't have died. They probably figured Jesus would heal Lazarus like He had so many others.

We stayed with them for a few days because they were so upset. Then four days later, Jesus finally showed up. I was visiting the cave where Lazarus was buried, so I saw Jesus coming up the road with a group of rough men. He didn't look like a prophet. One of Lazarus' sisters told Him He should have been there. If He had, Lazarus wouldn't have died.
Jesus said something really strange.

Jesus: I am the resurrection and the life. He who believes in me will have life even if he dies.

Narrator: I couldn't believe my ears. Only God gives life. How could this man be the resurrection and life? And how can we live if we die? That just doesn't make sense. Well, let me tell you, I was angry. First, He doesn't come to heal His friend or at least be there for Martha and Mary. Then He doesn't even come to the funeral. Then He says all this strange stuff about being the life.
But what happened next was amazing. Jesus told some men to roll the stone away from the cave door. I couldn't believe my ears.

(Have men roll stone away.)

After four days, the body would be decayed. They tried to tell Him that the body would stink, but He wouldn't listen. So, Martha and Mary had some men roll the stone away. And let me tell you, it did stink. I've never smelled anything so bad. It almost made me gag. I would have left, but I wanted to see what Jesus was up to, so I moved away until I could stand the smell.

Jesus: (Jesus walks up to the cave.)

Narrator: Jesus walked up to the opening in the cave. He must have had a strong stomach. Either that, or he couldn't smell anything. Then in a loud voice, He said something.

Jesus: (shouts) Lazarus, come forth.
Lazarus: (Lazarus comes out of the cave wrapped in toilet paper.)

Narrator: Amazing. Lazarus came back to life. Jesus told us to release him from his grave clothes. (Unwraps Lazarus.) We had a big party to celebrate. I'd like to hear more about this Jesus. If He can bring people back to life, maybe He is who He says He is. Maybe He's the Messiah, the one sent from God who has been promised.

Praise and Worship: Choose a couple of fast songs and a slow song to lead children into praise and worship. You can have a children's praise team, but until they understand leading praise and worship, have an adult leader or you be the worship leader.

Object Lessons:

1. Jesus Promises Eternal Life

Supplies Needed: A product that carries a lifetime guarantee. Some that come to mind are Tupperware®, Rubbermaid®, Craftsman® hand tools.

Show product to the children. Last week I went to the store and bought a new hammer (or whatever product you chose). Do you know why I bought this particular hammer? It is because it is guaranteed forever. The guarantee on this hammer says, "If this tool ever fails to provide complete satisfaction, return it for free repair or replacement."

That is great, isn't it? If I ever break this hammer, all I have to do is take it back to the store and they will either fix it or give me a new hammer.

Wait a minute! What if I lose my hammer? This guarantee doesn't say they'll replace the hammer if I lose it. What if someone steals it? I guess if I lose my hammer, or someone breaks into my garage and steals it, I'm out of luck.

Wouldn't it be great if something was guaranteed to last forever—and was guaranteed that you couldn't lose it and nobody could steal it? Well, there is!

Jesus promised everlasting life to those who trust and believe in Him. Listen to His guarantee!

John 10:28 (NIV) "I give them eternal life, and they shall never die!"

Does that guarantee that no one can steal it? It sure is!

In verse 29, Jesus said, "No one can snatch them out of my hand."

That means, if you believe in Jesus and trust Him as your Savior, you have eternal life and no one else can take it away as long as you continue to believe in Jesus. That's a guarantee that no one can match.

2. Object Lesson: Jesus Alone Has Eternal Life

Supplies needed: backpack

When you go to school, you have to make a lot of choices. What are some of the choices you make when you go to school?

Allow time for the children to answer, but if they don't respond, here are some suggestions to get them started.

One of the first things you will have to choose is what you will wear to school. That is pretty important, isn't it? After all, you want to look your best and make a good impression.

When you get to your classroom, you will have to choose where you want to sit. Is it best to sit up front, at the back, or maybe somewhere in the middle?

When it is time for lunch, you will have to choose what you want to eat in the cafeteria. Will you choose chicken nuggets or pizza?

Some choices you have to make are not very important. It doesn't matter if you wear your blue shirt today and your red shirt tomorrow or the other way around. If you have chicken nuggets today, you can have pizza tomorrow. Other decisions are very important. For instance, there are rules in your classroom. You have to choose whether you are going to follow the rules. If you decide not to follow the rules, you'll have to suffer the consequences.

You also choose who your friends are. That is important, because if you choose the wrong kind of friends, they might lead you into a lot of trouble.

The followers of Jesus faced some difficult decisions too. Sometimes, the teachings of Jesus were hard for them to understand. One day Jesus was teaching in the synagogue, and He said to the people, "I am the living bread that came down from heaven. Anyone who feeds on me will live forever." When the people heard it, they said, "This is a hard teaching. How can anyone accept it?" Some of them quit following Jesus after that day.

Jesus knew that many people were grumbling and complaining, so He turned to the twelve whom He had chosen to be His disciples and said, "You don't want to leave too, do you?"

Peter answered him. "Lord, to whom shall we go? You have the words of eternal life. We believe and know that you are the Holy One of God." The disciples had answered the call to follow Jesus. They had made the right decision, and they were not about to turn back now even if others did.

You and I face the same decision those first disciples faced. Will we follow Jesus, or will we look for another to lead us? It may not always be easy to follow Jesus, but to whom can we go? Who else offers eternal life?

Message: Ways to Get Eternal Life

Supplies needed: spray bottles and cleaning products labeled: giving, being good, going to church, reading Bible, praying, praising. Picture of Jesus or cross

(Use Journey to Resurrection Day Lesson 1, Slide 13.)

There are many ways people try to get eternal life. Some people give a lot of money. (Show giving bottle) It's good to give, but that won't give you eternal life.

Some people are good. (Show being good bottle) But nobody can be good enough all the time. That won't get you eternal life.

Some people read their Bibles every day. (Show reading Bible bottle) Reading your Bible is important, but it won't get you eternal life.

Some people pray or praise thinking God will be pleased with them if they do. (Show praying and praising bottles) God is pleased when we pray to Him and praise Him, but that won't get you eternal life.

(Show Lesson 1 Slide 1) John 11:25 (NIV) Jesus said…, "I am the resurrection and the life. The one who believes in me will live, even though they die;"

Believing in Jesus is the only way to have eternal life. If we accept Him as our Savior, we can live in Heaven with Him forever. We will have life even if we die.

Invite those children who want to accept Jesus as their Savior to come forward. Lead them in the sinner's prayer. Encourage these students that the prayer they repeated doesn't mean anything. What's important is praying to Jesus from your heart and surrendering your life to Him. You may want to meet with those children after service to explain more about salvation.

Here's an example of a sinner's prayer:

Lord Jesus, please forgive me of everything I've done wrong. I give my life to You. Come into my life, and be my Savior and Lord so that I can have eternal life. In Jesus' Name, Amen.

Small Group Activity: *Resurrection Chain Craft*

Supplies Needed: strips of construction paper in Easter colors, glue

Preparation: You can print out the verse for each strip below using Journey to Resurrection Day Media Resources. Glue the papers onto the construction paper strips.

Make a *Resurrection* chain countdown by having the children glue strips of construction paper together in loops. Use one loop for each day until Easter. On the last seven strips have children glue papers from the list below. Encourage students to hang the chain in their house or room and to read the strips each day with their families.

Here is a list of the strips to glue on the construction paper strips.

Passover Sunday:

Jesus entered Jerusalem and the people waved palm leaves and shouted, "Hosanna to the Son of David! Blessed is he who comes in the name of the Lord!"

Cleansing the Temple

Jesus went to the temple and drove out all who were buying and selling there. "It is written," he said to them, "My house will be called a house of prayer, but you are making it a den of robbers."

Teaching the People

Jesus spent time teaching the people to have faith, repent, and be baptized. He healed the sick and cared for the people. Children shouted, "Hosanna" when they saw Jesus!

Passover

Jesus held a Passover dinner with His disciples. He taught the disciples to have bread and wine to remember His sacrifice for them. That was the first communion.

Gethsemane

Jesus and eleven of His disciples went to the Garden of Gethsemane. Jesus prayed and asked God to help Him. Jesus said that He would do God's will and die for the sins of the world.

Good Friday

Jesus was arrested, beaten and crucified between two thieves. Jesus said, "Forgive them, for they know not what they do!"

Disciples

The disciples were afraid they would be arrested too. They deserted Jesus and hid. During Jesus' trial, Peter denied knowing Him. They didn't understand what would happen on Easter.

Easter Sunday, Resurrection Day!

Jesus rose from the grave. His friends visited His tomb and found the stone had been rolled away. An angel told them, "He is not here, for he is risen!"

Lesson 2: Jesus Enters Jerusalem (Palm Sunday)

Focus Point: God wants children to praise Him.

Goal: Students will learn that on Palm Sunday, Jesus encouraged children to praise Him. Today, He still wants the praises of children.

Verse of the Day: Matthew 21:16 (NIV) ... *From the lips of children and infants you, Lord, have called forth your praise?*

Supplies Needed:

- Journey to Resurrection Day Media Resources
- Bible costumes for skit (optional)
- Pin the Tail on the Donkey Game
- Paper cut in the shapes of palm branches
- Large palm branches (optional)
- Small Table
- Rocks
- Construction paper
- Craft (popsicle) sticks
- Scissors

Opening: Use Journey to Resurrection Day Slide or Countdown (Available free with registration of this curriculum.)

Welcome: Welcome the children. Wave your hands in the air and shout "Hosanna." Today is a very special day. It's Palm Sunday. When Jesus entered Jerusalem, everyone waved palms and shouted, "Hosanna." Each of you have two palms in your hands. Let's wave them and shout "Hosanna" in honor of Palm Sunday.

Prayer: Ask a child to pray over the service.

Rules: (use rules slide available in Journey to Resurrection Day Media Resources) Go over the 5 Ups Rules.

Go over the 5 Ups Rules:

- Sit up straight.
- Listen up.
- Hush up.
- Don't get up and run around or go to the bathroom without permission.
- Worship Up! (stand up and participate during praise and worship)

Theme or Activity Songs: Choose one or two fast-moving activity or theme songs that go with the curriculum.

Game Time: Pin the Tail on the Donkey (use game time slide)

Supplies Needed: Pin the Tail On the Donkey game

You can buy a "Pin the Tail on the Donkey" game at any party or toy store. The Internet also has instructions on how to make one.

After playing the game a few times, talk to the children about how Jesus rode to Jerusalem on a donkey.

Game Time (Optional): Palm Branch Limbo (use game time slide)

Supplies Needed: Palm branches

To play "Palm Branch Limbo," you will need a few palm branches. These branches are easily found in department stores and floral shops in the weeks leading up to Palm Sunday.

The children will have to limbo under the palm branches while the other children around them cheer them on.

Remind the children of how palm branches were placed in front of Jesus as the crowd around Him cheered Him on and shouted praises to Him.

Offering: Giving What We Have

On Palm Sunday, as Jesus rode into the city on a donkey, the crowd worshipped Him with what they had. They gave branches, coats, and praise because they loved Jesus and wanted to honor Him.

When we give our offering, we're honoring and worshipping Jesus! We're saying, "Jesus, You're our King, and we love You!"

You don't have to be rich or have a lot—just give what you have, like the people did on Palm Sunday.

Verse of the Day: Matthew 21:16 (NIV) … From the lips of children and infants you, Lord, have called forth your praise?

Memory Verse Skit: (Use Journey to Resurrection Day Lesson 2 Puppet Skit)

Simon: (comes out shouting) *Hosanna, hosanna. Today is Palm Sunday. When Jesus entered Jerusalem everybody shouted and praised God. But it wasn't only the adults praising. The children made such a ruckus that the temple leaders got angry. They told Jesus to stop the children from shouting praise. But Jesus wouldn't do it. He said in Matthew 21:16, (NIV) … From the lips of children and infants you, Lord, have called forth your praise? Jesus wants* *children to praise Him. That includes all of you. Hosanna.* (Shouts Hosanna as he leaves then keeps popping up to shout Hosanna.)

Memory Verse Talk: (use Journey to Resurrection Day Lesson 2, slide 1)

In many churches, adults stand and praise God during praise and worship time, but children sit and color or draw pictures. It's as if they don't feel like they're old enough to worship. But that's not how Jesus feels. Jesus wants to include children in praise. In fact, that's what today's memory verse is all about. In Matthew 21:16 (NIV), Jesus told the church leaders, "… From the lips of children and infants you, Lord, have called forth your praise?" Jesus wants children to worship Him. In fact, children worshipping is more powerful and important than adults worshipping. Let's worship God today. Lead children in shouting, "Hosanna."

Memory Verse Activity: Palm Verse Scramble

Supplies needed: paper cut in the shapes of palms (Use Lesson 2 Palm template in Journey to Resurrection Day.)

Preparation: cut papers in the shapes of palm branches and write each word of the verse on one palm. Have two sets, one each for two teams.

Lay the palm branches scattered on the floor in two areas. Have two teams of 3 to 5 children. Have them race to place the palm branches in order to show the memory verse.

Bible Story Skit: Jesus Enters Jerusalem (Use Journey to Resurrection Day Lesson 2 Bible Story Skit or have your drama team act this out.)

(Matthew 21:1-17)

Supplies Needed: Bible costumes, palm branches, small table

Narrator – Dressed in robe and turban

Jesus – Wears white robe

2 Children

Pharisee – Dressed in robe and turban

Narrator: Shalom everyone. That means peace. It's a greeting where I come from in Israel. In case you don't remember me from last week, I'm Simon. And I have a story to tell you. Remember how I told you Jesus raised Lazarus from the dead? This week He's riding into Jerusalem on a donkey like a king, and I hear everyone's bringing palm branches to wave at Him and yelling 'Son of David.'

Here He comes. Let's get our palm branches ready. Everyone wave, and yell Hosanna.

Jesus: (comes from the back)

Narrator: (encourages everyone to yell Hosanna and wave palm branches.)

Jesus: (goes to the temple.)

Narrator: That was exciting. But wait until you hear what happened next. When Jesus got to the temple, He was mad because some men were selling outside and cheating the people. He knocked over the tables.

Jesus: (knocks over the table) It is written, my house will be called a house of prayer. You have made it into a den of thieves.

Children: (come up to Jesus and wave palms) Hosanna, Son of David.

Pharisee: Do you hear what those children are saying? Tell them to be quiet.

Jesus: Have you never heard the scripture, "From the lips of children and infants you, Lord, have called forth your praise?"

Narrator: Jesus wants children to praise Him. Most people in Jerusalem want children to be seen and not heard. But not Jesus. I can't wait to see what's going to happen next.

Object Lessons:

1. Object Lesson: Palms

Supplies Needed: None

When Jesus entered Jerusalem, children and adult grabbed palm branches to praise Him with.

We don't always have palm branches around, but we can still praise Jesus with our palms. (Hold up your hands.) God created us with two palms we can always use to praise Him. Let's hold up our palms now and shout "Praise the Lord."

2. Object Lesson: Words for Praise

Supplies needed: Journey to Resurrection Day Lesson 2 Slides 2-12

Did you know there are different ways to praise God in the Bible? There are many different Hebrew praise words that talk about different ways to praise God. Here are some of them.

- Tehillah (pronounced tehela) To sing our praise to God with all our hearts.

- Zamar (pronounced zamar) To use instruments to show praise.

- Shabach (pronounced shabak) To shout.

- Halal (pronounced halal) To celebrate, go mad over, or to be clamorously foolish. Similar to a celebration at a sporting event.

- Machowl (pronounced machowil) To turn, skip, move around, lift the feet in dance.

- Towdah (pronounced toda) To extend the hands in acceptance or agreement with God's words and promises before you see the answer.

- Yadah (pronounced yada) To lift the hand in praise.

- Sachaq (pronounced sawqua) To laugh.

- Guwl (pronounced gool) To dance or spin.

- Alats (pronounced awlais) To let out a battle cry.

This is a good time to lead into Praise and Worship. Encourage the children to praise God the way some of these words suggest.

Praise and Worship: Choose a couple of fast songs and a slow song to lead children into praise and worship. You can have a children's praise team, but until they understand leading praise and worship, have an adult leader or you be the worship leader.

3. Object Lesson: The Rocks Cry Out

Supplies Needed: rocks

If you have enough rocks, give a rock or pebble to each child to take home. Tell them to put it out some place to remind them to praise the Lord.

Have any of you ever heard a rock talk? After the Pharisees tried to get Jesus to stop the children from praising Him, Jesus said something very interesting. He said if we don't praise Him, the rocks will cry out praise.

(Show the rocks) Have any of you ever heard a rock speak? That was amazing what Jesus said.

But if children hadn't praised Him as the Messiah the day He entered Jerusalem, that's just what would have happened. Rocks not only would have spoken, they would have cried out praises to God.

God wants His children to praise Him. He doesn't want to make the rocks praise because children won't. I don't want the rocks to cry out my praise. I want to praise God with my own mouth.

Let's do that right now. On the count of three, let's all shout "Praise the Lord".

Message: Ordained Praise

(Use Lesson 2 Slide 1

Quote the memory verse for today's lesson.

Matthew 21:16 (NIV) ... From the lips of children and infants you, Lord, have called forth your praise?

When Jesus said this, He said it in Hebrew. It was written down in Greek. And we quote the verse in English. What the verse really meant in the original language is that God taught children and babies to lead praise. That means that Jesus not only wants children to praise Him, He wants children to lead praise.

Have you ever seen a church that had children lead praise and worship in Big Church? Most churches normally have adults leading praise, but God wants children to lead praise. That doesn't mean you have to join the adult praise team. But it does mean, if you praise God with your whole heart, adults will see it and want to praise God too.

Ask the children to make a decision to praise God with their whole hearts. For altar time, lead them in some worship song and encourage them to praise God with their whole hearts. Before the worship, tell the students they can expect to feel the presence of God while they're worshipping. This means they might laugh, or cry, or they might fall down or lay on their faces. They might start speaking in a different language. Different things might happen, but even if those things don't happen, they feel the peace of God inside.

After the altar time, ask the children if they felt anything or if God spoke to them. By doing this, you're teaching them to be aware of God's presence when they worship.

Small Group Activity: Palm Praise Craft

Supplies Needed: construction paper, craft (popsicle) sticks, scissors

Have children trace their handprints onto construction paper. Have them cut out the handprints and glue them onto the craft sticks.

We made these palm branches to remind us that we all have palms to wave when we praise the Lord.

Lesson 3: Jesus Dies, Is Buried, & Rises Again

Theme: Jesus Wants Us to Be Saved

Verse: 1 Corinthians 15:3-4 (NIV) … Christ died for our sins according to the Scriptures, he was buried, he was raised on the third day according to the Scriptures.

Supplies Needed:

- colored Easter eggs
- bucket
- video of Jesus dying on the cross
- thunder special effects (You can find it on YouTube or a music subscription.)
- cave or tent
- temple curtain or small piece of cloth
- pictures or objects that symbolize the following: Easter egg, chocolate Easter bunny, candy, Easter basket, Easter bunny, flowers or something that symbolizes spring, Easter clothes, church bulletin, cross.
- Plastic Easter eggs with prizes and candy
- Plastic Easter egg for story

Opening: Use Journey to Resurrection Day Slide or Countdown (Available free with registration of this curriculum.)

Welcome: Welcome the children by saying, "He is risen." Explain to them that this was the greeting Christians used in the early days. Whenever somebody said, "He is risen," people would respond, "He is risen indeed." Tell the children that whenever you say, "He is risen," you want them to say, "He is risen indeed." Throughout the service today, say, "He is risen" and encourage the children to respond.

Prayer: Ask a child to pray over the service.

Rules: (use rules slide available in Journey to Resurrection Day Media Resources) Go over the 5 Ups Rules.

Go over the 5 Ups Rules:

- Sit up straight.
- Listen up.
- Hush up.
- Don't get up and run around or go to the bathroom without permission.
- Worship Up! (stand up and participate during praise and worship)

Theme or Activity Songs: Choose one or two fast-moving activity or theme songs that go with the curriculum.

Game: Easter Egg Relay

Supplies needed: colored Easter eggs, bucket

This is a relay game. Divide children into two teams. Have them roll Easter Eggs with their noses or have them run the relay with an egg under their chin and drop it in a bucket without breaking it. The team with the most unbroken eggs in the bucket wins.

Offering: Jesus Gave Everything

Jesus didn't just talk about love—He showed it when He gave His life for us on the cross, and then He rose again so we could have eternal life! That's the greatest gift anyone has ever given.

Because Jesus gave everything for us, we want to give back to Him—not just our money, but our hearts, our time, and our love.

When you give your offering today, remember: You're giving to say "Thank You, Jesus!" for all He's done.

Verse of the Day: 1 Corinthians 15:3-4 (NIV) … Christ died for our sins according to the Scriptures, he was buried, he was raised on the third day according to the Scriptures.

Memory Verse Puppet Skit: (use Journey to Resurrection Day Lesson 3 puppet skit)

Simon: *I'm so excited. Today is Resurrection Day. Did any of you receive Easter baskets? I did. I got lots of candy and a giant chocolate cross.*

But there's something even greater about Easter than candy. It's in our memory verse for today. 1 Corinthians 15:3-4 (NIV) says… Christ died for our sins according to the Scriptures, he was buried, he was raised on the third day according to the Scriptures.

On Good Friday, Jesus died for everything I ever did wrong so that I could have eternal life, and on Easter, He rose from the grave showing He is Lord and God and has power over everything, even death. He is risen.

Memory Verse Talk: The Gospel

When people use the word Gospel, it means good news. The Gospel of Jesus Christ is the best news ever. Our verse today tells the good news in one verse. Christ died for our sins. That means when we give our lives to Jesus, He has already taken the punishment for every wrong thing we've ever done. He died for us and was buried. But it doesn't end there. On the third day, Jesus rose from the grave, showing He is more powerful than sin, death, or the grave. We can put our faith in Him.

Memory Verse Activity: Ball Toss

Supplies needed: Ball

Have your students stand in a circle. Have them repeat the verse several times. Have each student bounce a ball to another student. Whenever a student catches the ball, he should say the verse. Continue until every student has a turn.

Bible Story Skit: Jesus Dies on the Cross and Rises Again

(Use Journey to Resurrection Day Lesson One Bible Story Skit or have your drama team act this out.)

Supplies needed (optional): Thunder special effects, cave or tent, Journey to Resurrection Day Lesson 3 Slide 2

Narrator – Dressed in robe and turban
Jesus – Wears white robe

Narrator: *It has been quite a week. I told you last week how Jesus came to Jerusalem. He claimed to be the Son of God. The religious leaders didn't like that. They had Him arrested. He was tried and executed. It was a very sad day for all of those who followed Him.*
(Show Journey to Resurrection Day Lesson 3 Slide 2.)

That happened three days ago. It was a sad day. I don't mind telling you I started believing Jesus was the Messiah, the Son of God. But now that He's dead, I guess it's over. I've been sitting here near His tomb. I don't know why. The religious leaders must have been right.

(Play thunder sound effects.)

What was that? I hear something.

Jesus: (emerges from the cave)

Narrator: *Did you see that? He's alive. Jesus rose from the grave. He is the Son of God.* (bows at Jesus' feet)

Object Lessons:

1. The Curtain Was Torn

Supplies Needed: Curtain set up so it can easily be torn in two. If you don't have a curtain, use a small piece of cloth.

In Bible days, Jerusalem had a temple with a great curtain. This curtain hid the Ark of the Covenant. The Ark was a gold box that showed God is with us always.

But the curtain kept people away from God. That's because sin keeps us from being close to God.

But Jesus died for our sins. He wants us to be close to God.

When He died on the cross, the curtain hiding the Ark of the Covenant was ripped in two like this. (rip the curtain or cloth)

That's because Jesus took the punishment for our sins. Now we don't have anything separating us from God. God wants us to be close to Him. All we have to do now is accept Jesus as our Savior from sin.

2. What Easter Is About

Supplies Needed: pictures or objects that symbolize the following: Easter egg, chocolate Easter bunny, candy, Easter basket, Easter bunny, flowers or something that symbolizes spring, Easter clothes, church bulletin, cross.

(You can also use Journey to Resurrection Day Lesson 3 Slides 3-8)

Show the objects as you say the following.

When most children think about Easter, they think about a lot of things. Some children like to color Easter eggs and have Easter egg hunts. (Show Easter egg or Slide 3)

Some children think about getting a gigantic chocolate Easter bunny or candy in their Easter baskets on Easter Sunday morning. (Show chocolate Easter bunny and Easter basket or Slide 3)

Then of course, there's the Easter bunny. (Show Easter bunny or Slide 4)

Spring break at school is usually around Easter. Some children think about spring and how they get to play outside more. (Show something that symbolizes spring or Slide 5)

Still other children's parents always buy them a new outfit they can wear to church on Easter. (Show new outfit. If one of the children has a special Easter outfit, have him or her model it or Slide 6.)

Some families only go to church on Easter. (Show church bulletin or picture of a church or Slide 7.)

All these things make us think about Easter. But the most important thing to think about on Easter is that Jesus died for our sins. (Show cross or Slide 8.)

Three days later, on Easter Sunday, He rose again. That's the best part about Easter. He died to save us from our sins, but He showed His power over death and rose again so that we could have eternal life. Jesus is not only our Savior, He's our Lord and King. He is risen!

3. The Colors of Easter

Supplies Needed: different colored plastic or real Easter eggs or different colored jellybeans.

Here are meanings you can teach children for colors associated with Easter.

Yellow: Radiance of Jesus who is the light of the world.

Green: Nature, Life, Jesus is the resurrection and the life.

Red: The blood of Jesus

White: Sins are washed away, Purity

Pink: Red and white together make pink. Jesus' blood washed our sins away.

Purple: Royalty, Jesus is the King of Kings.

Blue: Sky – Jesus ascended to Heaven

Story: The Empty Egg

Author unknown. This story has been told for years and is reported to be a true story although nobody knows where it came from.

Supplies Needed: plastic Easter egg

Many times at Easter, we decorate eggs and have Easter egg hunts. I'm going to tell you a true story about a little boy who understood what Easter is all about.

Jeremy Forester was born with a twisted body, a slow mind and a chronic, terminal illness that slowly killed him all his young life. Still, his parents had tried to give him as normal a life as possible and had sent him to St. Theresa's elementary school. At the age of twelve, Jeremy was only in second grade, seemingly unable to learn.

His teacher, Doris Miller, often became exasperated with him. He would squirm in his seat, drool and make grunting noises. At other times, he spoke clearly and distinctly, as if a spot of light had penetrated the darkness of his brain. Most of the time, however, Jeremy irritated his teacher. One day, Doris called his parents and asked them to come to St. Teresa's for a consultation. As the Foresters sat quietly in the empty classroom, Doris said to them, "Jeremy really belongs in a special school. It isn't fair to him to be with younger children who don't have learning problems. Why, there is a five-year gap between his age and that of the other students!"

Mrs. Forrester cried softly into a tissue while her husband spoke. "Miss Miller," he said, "there is no school of that kind nearby. It would be a terrible shock for Jeremy if we had to take him out of this school. We know he really likes it here."

Doris sat for a long time after they left, staring at the snow outside the window. Its coldness seemed to seep into her soul. She wanted to sympathize with the Foresters. After all, their only child had a terminal illness. But it wasn't fair to keep him in her class. She had eighteen other youngsters to teach and Jeremy was a distraction.

Furthermore, he would never learn to read or write. Why spend any more time trying? As she pondered the situation, guilt washed over her.

"Oh God," she said aloud, "here I am complaining when my problems are nothing compared with that poor family! Please help me to be more patient with Jeremy."

From that day on, she tried hard to ignore Jeremy's noises and his blank stares.

19

Then one day he limped to her desk, dragging his bad leg behind him. "I love you, Miss Miller," he exclaimed, loudly enough for the whole class to hear. The other children snickered, and Doris's face turned red. She stammered, "Wh-why, that's very nice, Jeremy. Now please take your seat."

Spring came, and the children talked excitedly about the coming of Easter. Doris told them the story of Jesus, and then to emphasize the idea of new life springing forth, she gave each of the children a large plastic egg.

"Now," she said to them "I want you to take this home and bring it back tomorrow with something inside that shows new life. Do you understand?"

"Yes, Miss Miller!" The children responded enthusiastically—all except for Jeremy. He just listened intently; his eyes never left her face. He did not even make his usual noises.

Had he understood what she had said about Jesus' death and resurrection? Did he understand the assignment? Perhaps she should call his parents and explain the project to them.

That evening, Doris' kitchen sink stopped up. She called the landlord and waited an hour for him to come by and unclog it. After that, she still had to shop for groceries, iron a blouse and prepare a vocabulary test for the next day. She completely forgot about phoning Jeremy's parents.

The next morning, nineteen children came to school, laughing and talking as they placed their eggs in the large wicker basket on Miss Miller's desk. After they completed their math lesson, it was time to open the eggs.

In the first egg, Doris found a flower. "Oh yes, a flower is certainly a sign of new life," she said. "When plants peek through the ground we know that spring is here." A small girl in the first row waved her arms. "That's my egg, Miss Miller," she called out.

The next egg contained a plastic butterfly, which looked very real. Doris held it up. "We all know that a caterpillar changes and turns into a beautiful butterfly. Yes, that is new life, too." Little Judy smiled proudly and said, "Miss Miller, that one is mine."

Next Doris found a rock with moss on it. She explained that the moss, too, showed life. Billy spoke up from the back of the classroom. "My daddy helped me!" He beamed.

Then Doris opened the fourth egg. She gasped. The egg was empty! Surely it must be Jeremy's, she thought, and, of course, he did not understand her instructions. If only she had not forgotten to phone his parents. Because she did not want to embarrass him, she quietly set the egg aside and reached for another.

Suddenly Jeremy spoke up. "Miss Miller, aren't you going to talk about my egg?"

Flustered, Doris replied, "But Jeremy, your egg is empty!"

He looked into her eyes and said softly, "Yes, but Jesus' tomb was empty too!"

Time stopped. When she could speak again, Doris asked him, "Do you know why the tomb was empty?"

"Oh yes!" Jeremy exclaimed. "Jesus was killed and put in there. Then His Father raised Him up!"

The recess bell rang. While the children excitedly ran out to the school yard, Doris cried. The cold inside her melted completely away.

Three months later, Jeremy died. Those who paid their respects at the mortuary were surprised to see nineteen eggs on top of his casket ...all of them empty.

Message: What Easter Means

Jesus died on the cross for our sins. He took the punishment for everything we ever did wrong so that we could be close to God. He did that because He loves us. All we have to do is accept Jesus' free gift of salvation, and we are saved from our sins. Jesus is our Savior.

But He's not just our Savior. Jesus showed that He is God and that He has power over life and death when He rose from the dead on Easter. We can have eternal life in Heaven because Jesus is Lord over our lives. Because of this, Jesus isn't just our Savior, He's our Lord and King.

Invite any children who are not saved to ask Jesus to forgive their sins and be their Savior. Invite all the children to make a commitment to make Jesus their Lord and King and to give their *entire* lives to Him.

Small Group Activity: Easter Egg Hunt

Supplies Needed: plastic Easter eggs with prizes and candy inside

Have an Easter egg hunt after children's church. Hide plastic Easter eggs with candy or prizes inside. If the weather permits, you could hide them outside on the church lawn. If not, hide them in the room.

MEET THE AUTHOR

Pastor Tamera Kraft is a passionate children's evangelist and founder of **Revival Fire for Kids Ministry** dedicated to equipping churches to lead children into a radical relationship with Jesus Christ. With over thirty years of experience in Spirit-filled children's ministry, Tamera has served as a children's pastor, curriculum developer, revivalist, and mentor to leaders across the nation.

Her journey began in 1987 when she was appointed children's pastor at her local church in Ohio. Since then, she has received the **Shepherd's Cup Award** for lifetime achievement in children's ministry and has raised up generations of young believers—many now serving in ministry themselves.

Through Revival Fire for Kids, Tamera travels nationwide conducting children's revivals, training leaders, and offering her signature curriculum, **Building Pentecostal Foundations**, which teaches kids to walk in the power of the Holy Spirit. Her online coaching platform, **Ignite Kidmin**, provides online consultations and leadership development for Kidmin leaders.

Tamera is also a published author of Christian historical fiction and lives in Tennessee with her husband Rick. Her heart beats for revival—and for seeing children encounter God in life-changing ways.

www.ingramcontent.com/pod-product-compliance
Lightning Source LLC
Chambersburg PA
CBHW081726120626
46550CB00010B/3269